UNSETTLED SUBJECTS

UNSETTLED SUBJECTS

New Poems on Classic
American Literature

ALLEN STEIN

BROADSTONE

Library of Congress Control Number 2020938793

ISBN 978-1-937968-69-4

Cover Artwork, Winslow Homer
"Northeaster"
Metropolitan Musem of Art Collection

Broadstone Books
An Imprint of
Broadstone Media LLC
418 Ann Street
Frankfort, KY 40601-1929
BroadstoneBooks.com

Once again, for Connie

CONTENTS

Hester Prynne Gazes Homeward

(in England, Hester contemplates a return to Boston)

She sits at the window and stares to the west.
Through the settling mists she sees "Drake's Island,"
six acres of craggy hill and stunted tree
from which Sir Francis set out,
leaving this sound for less tranquil waters,
never so much at home
as when striding solid planks under swelling canvas.
She muses on that restless man,
picturing him gripping the stern-rail
as he watches sluggish Plymouth
slowly, too slowly, grow small to the north,
and then, for long hours, still at the rail,
gazing Land's End to a vanishing point in the east,
and at last turning, thrilling to know
that the New World and all beyond
lay now but an ocean's voyage ahead of his bow.

But Hester's gaze, this day, is due west from the start,
sweeping swiftly over the sound,
over Cornwall, over Land's End
and countless sea swells past,
to Massachusetts Bay's new Eden,
where her first sight of Arthur made her yearn
for a newer world still, one well west of Boston,
as fresh as newborn Eve woke to on that sixth dawn,
when her eyes blinked open and stared about in wonder.

She knows herself now no less eager than Drake
to sail from this place,
and, strangely, never so much at home
as when, like him, she trod oaken boards.
But these boards were not under sail,
but on scaffold, under pillory.

She perceives fully, at last,
that neither rocking at cottage hearth,

Pearl in her lap,
nor panting, stretched on leaf-bedded forest floor
beneath Arthur, his eyes straining with lust and guilt,
nor ever in all her days and nights since,
has she ever been more herself
than when she stood above the crowd,
and returned gaze for gaze,
silent, indurated, defiant.

Seven muted years after, on the scaffold once more,
she spoke.
His head at her bosom, Arthur, dying,
strained and panted now
only for his dream of heaven,
as Hester, bereft, yet again herself,
her face bent to his,
whispered that surely, surely their immortal life
would be spent together,
no matter the word of man or God,
no less certain than ever
that her will had its own consecration.
With such speech,
and the planks beneath her,
and the breeze from the bay bringing a fresh scent of salt,
Hester felt herself sailing far from all shores,
as if pillory were ship, and she its crew and captain,
seeking dark and distant waters
charting a course of no one's choosing but her own.

But for too long now, settled England has claimed her.
There is much that is not displeasing—
her Pearl's cheery English husband,
her doughty grandson's rosy English cheek,
the weathered bricks and well-trod garden paths
of their ancient and estimable house;
yet Pearl's domestic pliancy gives Hester little pleasure
as she looks to the faint shrouded glow in the west.

She will leave this land and not return.
Roger knew Necessity blossoms as it must,
that character follows its bent,
be it sinuous as serpent
or unswerving as Boston's sullen God.
And she will follow hers,
step ashore at her only true home,
take up her letter and her name,
speak again as Hester Prynne,
telling women of wondrous voyages
awaiting them in days somewhat less far off
than the horizon Drake unfailingly sought.

Such speech, she at once fears and hopes,
may bring her back to the boards of the scaffold—
this time to sail off them,
to unmapped spaces, her neck in a noose,
her penitence, so watched for by Boston in years past,
forever yet to be.
It's a voyage outward she feels no less meant for
than Sir Francis for his, as he stood at the dock's edge,
with thought of return the last thing on his mind.

Sophia Hawthorne Responds to Attacks on her Husband's Book

The questioning of its morality
is of all criticisms the funniest.
Indeed, the whole book is one great chorus
of condemnation,
as terrific and stunning as a thunderbolt,
proclaiming the Law cannot be broken.
Oh, it is a tale of such terrible retribution!
It troubles me.

As Mr. Hawthorne read me the final pages,
the ink still moist, that turbulent night,
his voice, swaying me like a mighty wind,
was tremulous with the pathos of God's Word
speaking through him.
Hester Prynne's profane passion had been a flame
that *would* not submit to the Divine will
(nor, it seemed, to Mr. Hawthorne's).
It had blazed as she lay with Mr. Dimmesdale.

Was it in her bedchamber or his?
In darkness or light?
Were curtains quivering in an evening breeze
that could not chill two bodies coiled in unholy heat
or did late afternoon sunshine,
palpitant with slowly swirling motes,
pour upon them through nearly closed shutters,
its glow reduced to mere dimness
as the pair burned brightly in their lust?
Perhaps it was on the floor of his study
or on a couch of forest leaves,
neither of them conscious of hard or soft,
save in what they felt in the other's hot flesh.

And her passion smoldered through seven years
of penance without penitence,

and compliance without contrition,
of wayward thoughts behind down-cast eyes,
till flaring once more,
it guttered and died on the scaffold,
extinguished at last by the breath of holiness
suffusing Arthur's final words,
suffusing the ink from my husband's pen,
leaving Hester chastened,
submissive as God and Mr. Hawthorne could demand.

Or was she still yearning
to feel his soft palms sliding across her skin,
the tips of her nails penetrating his?

I felt an ocean straining
to pour from my heart and eyes
as Mr. Hawthorne's voice, heaving and groaning,
subsided to whisper tremulously
of Hester's grave beside Arthur's.

I slept fitfully that night,
my dreams hectic as my pulse.
I saw Hester in bedroom, study, and on forest floor,
her parted lips moist with her licking,
her teeth bared and bright,
her eyes lit with license,
gazing upon her eager lover, my husband.

I awoke, perspiring and perplexed,
telling myself once more that the lesson
of Mr. Hawthorne's book is that
the Law CANNOT be broken!

THE NAMING OF HAWKEYE

"No fear *there*," the dying old brave said,
tapping with trembling finger the breast
of Deerslayer, the boy whose aim had been true.
Blood bubbled at his lip now
as he lay with his head in the boy's lap,
while the lad sat silent on a stone beside the water.
The brave stared up into the paleface's eyes,
blue and deep as this lake
to which Deerslayer had borne him
for a drink to soothe the bullet's searing.
Spraying flecks of red onto the boy's buckskin,
he said, "Eye certain, finger lightning, aim death.
You great warrior soon. Need new name."
He closed his eyes, considered,
then "Hawkeye, Hawkeye, Hawkeye,"
streamed out with the blood that ran down his chin,
and, finally, the command, "Shake hand!"
Hawkeye felt the hand go still even as he grasped it.

He set the dead man against the rock,
propped not to fall,
back upright, legs stretched straight,
his duty to leave the brave to his silent dignity.

Hawkeye leans now on his rifle and muses.
This is the first man he has killed,
the first he's raised his hand against.
Staring down at him, he says,
"I didn't wish your life, red-skin,
but you left me no choice
atween killing or being killed."

He sighs and looks out over the lake,
this placid Glimmerglass he loves,
watches the tiny whitecaps,
the glints of bobbing April sunshine,

and fears that his having to kill again
and then again
is a thing as certain as the passing of the seasons,
as the storms that churn these waters to darkness.

This destiny was manifest for him
the day white men first stepped onto the soil
of this continent, for his aim, as the dying warrior said,
is death, and history apparently will make much use of him.
He takes pride in his courage, in the keenness of his sight,
and is pained by this pride.

His unsullied innocence
is as precarious as the clear blue gleaming
of this lake in the path of the pioneers.

Innocence is as elusive as the setting sun
he will follow someday ever westward.

Still looking out over the quiet waters,
he feels a sob rising in his throat.
He swallows it back hard,
looks once more at the impassive visage
of the man he killed
and turns to leave,
eager to tell his old friend Chingachgook
all that he has done,
eager to take the old Mohican by the hand.

THE PASSING OF EDGAR POE

"There is a gentleman, rather the worse for wear,
at Ryan's 4th ward polling place,
who goes under the cognomen of Edgar A. Poe,
and who appears in great distress.
I assure you he is in need
of immediate assistance."

So read the letter to Poe's friend
from a concerned bystander
in the streets of Baltimore,
a local printer who had never set type
for a word penned by Poe,
but who knew pure anguish
when he saw it.

The friend, a physician,
saw merely its vestments:
a battered straw hat,
a stained coat of faded bombazine,
a filthy shirt, pants torn at the knee
and frayed at the ankle,
ill-fitting shoes
unpolished and down at the heels.
The clothes likely another's,
the pain doubtless his own.

His appearance, remarked the friend,
was "repulsive,"
evidence of "a state of beastly intoxication."
The eyes, "lusterless and vacant,"
were the sign and seal of it.

Alcohol is itself a vestment for a soul in terror.
What had brought him to this moment?
The proximate cause is uncertain.
(The death that followed,
four days later, is not.)

A drink or two in him,
he might, willingly or no,
have taken another and then another,
until long past willing or unwilling,
he became a "repeater,"
hauled from poll to poll,
to drink and vote
and drink and vote again,
under various guises,
till overcome by delirium,
he was unfit for even the 4th ward hacks.

This but the leading theory among many,
not implausible,
(and not without ironic appeal,
given that Poe saw the nation's politics
as only for the devious or delirious)
but, like the rest, not conclusive.

Yet even if a proximate cause were proven,
we yearn for more;
like Poe himself, we long for ultimates.

Why was he in Baltimore anyway?
Indeed, one might ask, as, no doubt, he often did,
why was he anywhere at all?

One must go back,
past Baltimore and its gutters,
and the train trip that for no discernible reason
deposited him there.

One must go past a sepulchre in a kingdom by the sea,
past a chilly cottage at Fordham
where a young wife lies freezing under blankets,
coughing till she hemorrhages,
past a chamber where a grieving man

broods over a volume of forgotten lore,
beyond a decaying house reflected in a turbid tarn,
and a walled pleasure-palace of maddest revelry
in a plague-ridden land.
And like the knight pursuing El Dorado,
one must not flag in the journey.
There's still the hard-packed dirt
of the parade ground at West Point,
the parapet of Fort Moultrie,
where a lonely recruit might lean and stare
through long nights at the waves sweeping
onto the sands of Sullivan's Island.
And farther back yet, at Jefferson's university,
there's the student's room on the Lawn,
its table holding playing cards and drink,
the Allan house in Richmond where a headstrong boy
was told too often to be grateful,
the cramped boardinghouse parlor in Boston
where a frail actress gave birth to the boy,
a lad with high forehead
and searching wary eyes.

But one mustn't stop even here.
One must push on farther,
just as in his last months did Poe himself,
to the Beginning of all.
Eureka, his "poem in prose," priceless
"for the Beauty that abounds in its Truth,"
though a mere 75 cents at the booksellers,
revealed the Source to be the Spirit Divine
at the core of cosmic silence.

Be it Helen of hyacinth hair and classic face,
grizzled old man with "vulture" eye,
the prematurely buried or those
who hastened them to the tomb,
all have their origin in the Spirit made palpable.

And destruction itself, by sacred design,
is but part of an ages-long "ingathering"
till each is absorbed into the Spirit
that was our genesis but never our end;
for again will occur the incarnation,
the expansion over eons,
till the next ingathering—
the dead undying,
the perished imperishable,
all pulsing in a Cosmic Heartbeat eternal,
throbbing beyond loss, beyond grief,
in the unending rhythmic creation of Beauty.

Why, then, after such revelation,
was his gaze "lusterless and vacant"?

There was always the terror,
that no euphoric prose poem
could will away for long,
the fear that at the beginning
there was only silence,
and that at the close
there will be only silence—
Spirit, Plan or Purpose
no more than a dream within a dream.
Helen, Lenore, Virginia Poe,
black cats and croaking ravens—
their lives random and inexplicable as his own,
as that of whatever created him,
random and inexplicable as horror itself.
One now has gone back as far as one can
from Ryan's in the 4th Ward,
as far back as Poe himself could go.

Poe, then, was at Ryan's
because that was where he happened to be.

There could be no assistance
for this gentleman in great distress,
at a polling place in Baltimore.

Virginia Poe Dying

"I see no one among the living
as beautiful as my little wife"—
words moist from the tip of Eddie's pen,
words written of me.
I watch as they mark with his love
the unstained white sheet upon his desk,
and I yearn to run my tongue softly across the nib,
to feel the ink, heated by his devotion,
slide along its pink, quivering surface
and far into my throat,
calming my blood-flecked coughs,
penetrating my throbbing veins
and warming my chilling sweat.

Soon I shall not be among the living,
and then Eddie will find me
more beautiful yet,
beyond the troublesome allure of touch,
translated to a vision,
a lovely unbodied ghost
cleansed by sweetest-saddest music
and swathed in highest, vaguest longings.

These last weeks he has lingered so attentively
at my bedside in our little wintry room,
his only cloak spread atop my blanket,
his gloved fingers often at my brow.
He smiles through the shivers he can't suppress
and seeks to assure us both that my hectic flush
bespeaks the return of radiant health.

Yet he will linger more attentively still
at my tomb,
as cold marble seems most pleasing to his touch.
Oh, I fear he would have loved me best as a statue,

one over which a dark bird might hover
and croak of the somber joys of endless yearning,
averring that 'nevermore' touches the soul
as 'evermore' cannot.

A forest trail leading to a mist-shrouded mausoleum,
a rocky path to a sepulchre by the sea,
these are the settings that speak to his spirit.

I blame him not,
only love him the more
for the purity of his ideal,
and yet . . .
did God clothe us in flesh
only to make us wish to flee it?
His sainted mother lost in her youth,
his unsullied bride of thirteen—
such stainlessness was all Eddie knew of woman
and all he cared to know.
So when, no longer thirteen,
I came to sense a woman's stirrings,
I remained the frail child-wife,
never seeking to beguile him
with sinuously stroking hands,
winsome words breathed softly at his ear,
or sly smiles showing red lips and bright teeth,
certain that he would flinch as if from a serpent
seeking to ensnare him in this squalid, mottled world,

Last Valentine's day
(truly, I fear, my last),
I composed verse of my own,
adoring words for my darling Eddie.
"Love," I wrote him,
"would heal my weakened lungs."
This, I perceive now, is not to be.
Perhaps instead our love has made me

too ethereal for this life,
too insubstantial to resent as did his Ligeia
the passing into mere vapor,
as impalpable as he doubtless wished me from the first.

In these last hours, I startle myself
thinking of men broad, brawny and lustful
and can scarce meet my dear haunted husband's soulful eyes.

Ralph Waldo Emerson Meets John Brown

He has insisted over the years
that nothing is at last sacred
but the integrity of one's own mind,
and in the lecture halls
the crowds gaze up at him
and, as one,
nod cheerily in vague agreement,
the flicker of the gaslight
making them seem substantial
as the shadows on the wall.

Each pair seated beneath him
is but one couple more.
Afterwards, they gurgle
that they've been "inspired,"
and simper in bovine complacency.

He has told them for years
that all Adam had,
all Caesar could,
each of them has and can do,
but he knows better now.
The loins of the republic are profligate,
but the beautiful is never plentiful.
He looks in vain for brain, spine, and spirit,
an answering eye.

Tonight, though, in his own parlor,
he meets eyes that fathom him
as he shakes the callused hand of John Brown
—Brown of Bleeding Kansas,
a man of a sort not plentiful,
who has met the dimming gaze of dying slavers,
men hacked open by a blood-smeared broadsword,
held in that hard palm
that now presses Emerson's own.

As if all were inevitable as the tides,
Brown says softly, "I will purge this land
with blood, ankle deep, if need be, sir,
till black bondage infects it no more.
And your words, sir,
are ever my beacon in this holy cause."

Freeing his hand, he asks,
"But all the killing, Mr. Brown—
surely one must quail at that prospect?"

"I give you back your own words, sir.
You have said that to look within
is to look above.
Thus I have done.
And I find myself suffused
with the very force of the indwelling Spirit.
My course is clear as Christ's."

"But how do you know it is holy?" he asks,
his eyes still meeting Brown's deep, measuring stare.
"I know because I know," is the response.
"This, as you of all men must perceive, is the way
of the self-reliant, the way of Truth.
You will join the battle, then?"

Emerson is uneasy, but has no rejoinder,
at least not while those eyes hold his.
A long moment passes,
and he looks away,
to the cheque book he has drawn from his pocket.

As he writes a tidy sum over to Brown,
he finds himself eager
to turn back to the lecture halls
and the mass of upturned gazes.

THOREAU, ROCKS, WALLS, AND PENCILS

I

Would any wish to work for his bread
by shying stones over a wall through morning,
and tossing them back all afternoon?
Thoreau posed the question,
and knew but one answer:
none would willingly take up a task
so feckless, so futile;
yet, he chides, many indeed
labor no more meaningfully,
earning daily the costly wages
of quiet desperation.

But at the wall one might scent pine and spruce,
damp grass and early wildflowers
in the sunrise air of April, and know the feel
of solid rock gripped in your palm,
of a pivot at the hip, a swing of the arm,
and the sight of what had been inert, perhaps for ages,
now soaring, glinting, clearing the barrier,
and landing with a substantial thud
or brisk clatter on the other side.
And so it would go as the sun rose higher
through the warming hours,
your muscles loosening, limbering,
your sleeves rolled above your elbows,
a light sweat gleaming at your forearms.
Then a lunch, eaten eagerly,
perhaps savory slabs of ham perfectly-cured,
a nutty cheese and pungent mustard,
between thick slices from a grainy loaf,
washed down with apple cider
cooled all morning in the chill brook nearby.
A catnap and then to the other side of the wall,
the side shielded from the day's hotter rays,

and the work beginning anew.
Once again the flinging of stone after stone,
the sweat coming more profusely now
as the afternoon passed quietly,
the only sounds the rustle of the boughs,
the landing of the rocks, and your own breathing,
strong and steady.
And just before quitting time the breeze quickening,
cooling a body warm and pleasantly weary
with the day's unwavering work.

And, yes, some days the sun might scorch
and mosquitos bite,
and on others an icy wind
might sting your face and shiver your spine,
but the job would end each evening
with the rocks moved away and then back,
where they'd wait for you tomorrow,
the solid stuff of your vocation.

Thoreau would ask, of course,
"To what purpose?"
How to answer him?
One might cite Carlyle's claim
that "Every idle moment is treason"
and let it go at that,
the assertion seeming sufficient unto itself.

Yet, from a certain perspective
(often Thoreau's),
all work is contemptible,
merely a shifting about of things,
or of numbers, papers, words—
all no more at best than improved means
to a wrong end.

Nonetheless, is it contemptible
to take satisfaction in stones well-hurled,
in barriers well-cleared?
Perhaps any work well-done
becomes at last its own end and purpose,
coherent in its own beauty
as a finer fruit of life,
a true assertion of one's presence.

Sisyphus, so some suggest,
smiled each time he struggled the boulder
to the crest,
and, but moments later,
smiled still as he strode downslope
to where it had settled once more,
as ever it must,
at the bottom.

II

Once, pencils made in America
were greasy, gritty and brittle.
Thoreau changed all that.
Grinding graphite finer
and mixing it with clay,
he produced a better pencil,
"superior in every respect
to any American pencils
I have yet met with,"
as one satisfied user among many,
a Mr. D.C. Johnston, declared.
Soon after, Thoreau stopped making pencils,
saying "I would not do again
what I have done once."

Making piles of pencils, superior or not,
mattered no more to Thoreau
than throwing from heap of stones
to heap of stones.

He claimed there is always new day to dawn,
that the sun is but a morning-star,
and that his land was the land
for fresh starts.
So one turn at pencil-making,
one sojourn in the cabin at the pond,
one night in jail,
each never to be repeated,
any more than a book is to be written again,
word for word, with even the finest of pencils
—all are part of the making of one life,
irreducibly one's own and no other's.

Nevertheless, when the sun, that morning-star,
dawns on each new day,
there are always more stones to be moved,
more pencils to be made,
and the need to do both well.

Thoreau on the Shore

"A man can attend but one funeral
in the course of his life,
can behold but one corpse."
So said Thoreau seeing the bodies,
twenty-eight in all,
laid out, rigid as pencils,
at Cohasset on Cape Cod,
gone down in the wreck of the *St. John*,
and awaiting near a hundred others
yet to wash in with the waves.

Having traveled much in quiet Concord,
he'd been eager for Provincetown
and his first look at surges and ebbs
and the ribbings of moist-packed sands,
open to the skies and the next tide.

But the handbills blaring the disaster
brought him to Cohasset
for a sight not to be missed.
And indeed there were things to see—
"many marbled feet and matted heads"
visible when the cloths were raised,
and one drowned girl in full view,
livid, mangled, swollen,
her eyes wide open and staring,
like those of fish on ice.

He found the scene not so "impressive"
as he might have expected.
Had there been but one body
cast upon the beach
in some lonely place,
he would have felt more, he said,
for it was the individual and the private
that claimed his affinity.

Multiplied corpses brought diminishing returns.
Though he could see
the whole possibility of the race,
as it were, in the one,
it was not his way to see
the ones in the many.
Thus, he said he "sympathized"
rather with the winds and waves,
for tossing and twisting bodies
divested of spirit
was their order of the day,
the law of Nature,
and they worked more effectually
than the mass of men ever can.

The first funeral, the first corpse,
Thoreau asserts,
offers conclusive education
in the matter of body and soul.
This world is but the rock
on which our ship foundered,
the strand on which our hulk
rots to nothing
while its cargo is guided
to a golden elsewhere
by a most "skillful pilot"
amidst fairest and balmiest breezes.
Other funerals, other corpses,
offer mere repetition of this sacred lesson.

Thus, he turned readily to metaphor
as he turned from the bodies on the beach.
But the sound of his flute floating
over the gentle waters of Walden,
the sight of his cabin sitting firm and sound,
on the land where he built it,

the taste of New England berries
gathered in breeze and sunshine,
indeed all the varied pleasures of his world,
though also the stuff of metaphor,
he savored as actualities and ever would
as he lived the life he valued as his own
and no one else's.

BARTLEBY'S LAST SPEECH

They found Bartleby laying huddled in the yard,
his forehead flush against the wall,
like he'd been trying to think through
to the other side
and then way past that.
Sad, but no surprise.
I saw what he was after when they brung him in,
and it wasn't to be here, or anywhere
that has dirt below and sky above.

Never had a cellmate so still and gray;
gave me most all his grub
and didn't care a stale crumb
whether I glommed it down or not,
just went on staring
at dead walls with near-dead eyes.

Last night, though, while he's watching the wall,
I says to the back of his head,
"Seems like eating don't agree with you."
He nods, but don't turn around none.
"And maybe," I says, "what don't agree even worse
is being near folks that's feeding?"
(He'd cringed hearing me tear into hard crusts.)
He faces me at that, his eyes lighting some,
but no brighter than a weak torch in a damp tomb,
his lips up at the corners the least bit,
like the undertaker fixes 'em on a corpse,
and he says softly, "You saw that, eh?"
"Yeah," I says, "you ain't got much appetite
 for appetite, looks like."
"No, not much," he tells me,
"and you're the first to see it.
Most prefer not to—
might trouble them as to causes."

With him dolloping out that much talk,
I figured his larder had gone just about bare,
but he had a healthy stock hoarded up.

Sitting himself down slow on the floor,
his back against the wall,
his face in the shadows,
he went on, his voice dull and flat,
"I've seen things, you know,
that gnaw at me still.
I've watched sharks churn the waters red,
ripping open the torn whale
and each other,
entrails hanging from their teeth.
Then, but hours later, I've watched men,
their jaws glistening with the thick grease of their meal,
greedily downing shark steaks done rare.
Think you, though, that such is merely the way of the sea?
Think again, for every living thing is at last diner or meal.
The stooped and scarred slaves of the field,
the haggard loom-girls of the factory,
the bent clerks peering red-eyed
at ledgers from their high stools
are swallowed as surely as the thin oat porridge they spoon
or the roast beef that yields to their masters' fork and blade.

"I took my final lesson in the way of the world
on Wall Street, that center of things as they are.
Within the walls of an attorney's chambers,
all gorged on what they could—such the law.
Apples, cakes, and ale fed
Turkey, Nippers, and Ginger-Nut,
who, in turn, fed our employer—
the three of them morsels
for the gaping maw of commerce.
Each hungered for higher station, only he achieved it.

As it is on that walled-in street,
so it is in this walled-in world.

"I preferred at last neither to feed nor to be fed upon—
thus to them a mystery,
a dead letter of illegible address.
Perhaps I might be deliverable elsewhere,
where all might be read clearly and lovingly—
of this, though, I have my doubts."

I nodded and told Bartleby with a smile
that in the brawl that brought me here again,
I bit deep into the nape of some copper's neck.

Bartleby smiled back, his teeth showing dim from the shadows,
and we preferred to speak no more.

The Last Musings of Malcolm Melville, His Father's Son

(Died by his own hand, at eighteen, September 11, 1867)

Of a Sunday morning, when I was but a boy,
Father would take me down to the Battery,
set his elbows on the wall, and stare out at the bay.
He seemed to require me simply as witness
to his dim brooding,
a ready stand-in for the readers
his broodings in print no longer brought him.

In truth, Father has always had most to say to me
through words on a page.
Seven years ago, he wrote from Tierra del Fuego
of a young sailor who fell from the rigging
to the deck below.
As the ship rolled and groaned
with every surge of the dark and heavy waves,
the corpse was placed on a plank,
the beleaguered captain mumbled a hurried prayer,
and then on his muttered command,
the plank was raised and tipped.
"The body slid away and we saw it no more.
Such is the way a sailor is buried at sea," said Father.
His next words were, "Now is the time to show what you are—
a good, honorable boy, or a good-for-nothing one."

Now, six days a week, at my desk,
landlocked at Great Western Marine Insurance,
I peer between walls of sooty buildings
toward the Battery and bay,
a clerk seeking to glimpse a sail
headed to parts unknown.
The letter sits in my desk drawer,
and each morning, six days a week,
I read it dutifully once more,
and just as dutifully serve
in the position Father secured for me,

here in the city,
ever safe, ever close to hand
for Mother and the youngsters,
a good, honorable boy,
while Father roams, seeking the wake of God,
searching with no less enraged longing
than Ahab's in following his white whale.
Father's topmost fear is that phantoms leave no wake,
and thus he broods in sullen silences
and murky seethings.

As a boy of seven, I wept
when he spoke harshly to my sister.
He placed his hand on my head,
the pressure of it making me bend at the knees,
and murmured, "Ah, Mackie, you're a soft one, are ye?
This world will prove unkind to you, I fear."

"The Dead of Antietam," covered the walls
as Father walked me through the charnel house
that was Brady's exhibit hall four years ago.
The photographed bodies, bloated and twisted,
looked dropped from the sky
to lie here in a bloody heap.
"Let this cleanse you early of illusions," Father said,
"as the sea cleanses the kelp of grit.
Ah, in no world but a fallen one could such things be."
(Fallen from what I did not ask.)
Leaving the hall, I walked with Father up Broadway,
his gait as always rolling slightly from side to side,
as if he were striding the length of a struggling ship,
his shoulders hunched as if anticipating a blow.

Two months past, Sunday, he flung me against the wall
when I cried "Before God, Father, it's not right!"
and grabbed at his arm
to keep him from striking Mother.

As I lay where I fell in our parlor,
I stared at a framed print above me
that now hung wildly askew,
making those in it, clinging to their makeshift raft
from the wreck of the *Medusa*,
seem imminently to slip from it
into the bottomless dark and troubled sea.
The blackened sky toward which they stared
through the vacant distance
rose looming with the off-kilter frame
till it seemed ready to cover all forever.
"No, Mackie," Father said softly,
as he turned from me and Mother,
"it's not right. Before God or Godlessness, it is not."
Mother's going to church that morning
had provoked him to raise his hand against her.

Tonight, I entered Father's study,
my bearing erect, a proud grin on my face.
"Father, I have joined the Guard," I proclaimed.
He sighed, put down his pen, turning to me from his page,
and said quietly, "'*Pro patria mori*,' is it, Mackie?
Is Moloch thirsting still for young blood?
Are the bedraggled Mexicans and the three millions of Canada
eager to sweep across our borders
and contend with the thirty millions of America?
Or perhaps you see new internal conflicts brewing, Mackie?"
"Yes, perhaps internal ones," I said, finally,
as abashed as any of the *Pequod's* crew before inscrutable Ahab,
my head bent, my eyes downcast,
my eagerness for military dress and drilling
seeming suddenly as boyish and bootless
as my early dreams of brave voyages and manly ventures.
I left him silently,
my gait rolling, my shoulders hunched.

Hours later now, I lie in my bed.
The time till dawn passes slowly
as I roll the cylinder of my new Colt,
three of its six chambers filled.
If there is a God, He will let me live—
live that I may prove myself
truly good and honorable.

If there be none, then my futile hopes
for here and hereafter must drop
like a sailor fallen from the rigging.
I whirl the cylinder and put the barrel to my temple.
Perhaps I rise in the morning
to hear church bells tolling the hours of holy Sabbath,
or perhaps I shall be found hearing nothing,
merely offering Father a fresh blank page.

THE APOLOGIA OF JOHN CLAGGART, MASTER AT ARMS OF THE *BELLIPOTENT*

I died for Billy, body and blood,
died that his name would live.
Welkin-eyed Billy, stammering boy,
I knew if the cannon didn't kill him,
the quimhouses would.
And if he'd gone down by mere shot or syph,
burst ope' or blotched with pox,
who'd then have sung of Billy Budd?

You see, even I can't speak of Billy now
without near breaking into ballad or hymn.

I leave such songs to others, though.

It's a man o' war's world, after all—
though brightsome Billy never knew.
So lacking ragged edges,
so senseless of the scorpion's sting—
such innocence is culpable,
naught but careless cheer,
except it be put to purpose.
And my foregone purpose was to give him his.

The times, like all times, were restive,
and roiling waters must be calmed.
No need of policemen in Heaven,
yet here we hire Masters-at-Arms.
Christ hoped his cross sufficient,
still true peace calls for the noose.

I knew I could trust charming Billy
to bless Vere and die with a smile,
thus prompting the murmuring echo,
the rabble's sighing submission,
their dumb fealty to station and measure,
dumb fear of the Order that smites.

Seeing his look as he struck me,
his words too stifled to speak,
was at once my agony and recompense,
and I died with my purpose complete.

While, lashed in my hammock,
dark fathoms down and down,
I lay tangled in oozy weeds,
Billy ascended in the full rose of dawn,
and swayed freely in the breeze.
The birds croaked their requiem,
the crew loosed their tears,
sad brutes redeemed for a time,
to the service of their Ruler Divine.

Like Jesus, Billy rose to glory
that men would drop to the knee.
Like Judas, I chose the harder way,
that our Father's will be done.

Herman Melville, Customs Inspector Number 188

(From 1866 to 1886, Melville, unable to earn a living through his
writing, worked as a customs inspector for the City of New York)

A salt spray dampens his cheek,
as the deck sways beneath him.
He walks the oaken boards
no less steadily than he did decades before,
and the chill breeze warms him with memories.
But the furled sails and the slack hawsers
looped firmly 'round the pier's bollards
remind him that ahead of the bow
are not open seas, scudding clouds,
and the Marquesas of his youth
but Manhattan and its scrum of streets,
its spires, and its dead walls.

He holds no whaleboat oar nor cutting spade now,
merely ledger and pen,
and instead of sturdy, weathered gray tarpaulin,
wears a blue uniform, faded with innumerable brushings,
and badge 188, tarnished with twenty years
of reading lading lists and taking inventory.
(He suspects he looks like a doorman
at a hotel no longer fashionable.)
A lingering glance at the sky, and he goes below,
walks among barrels of coffee beans,
crates of bananas, kegs of rum,
and inks entries in his ledger's tight lines
as with each breath he catches the scent
of the tropics he'll see no more.

Back on deck, he has a mad impulse
to scramble up the mainmast
and rest in the rigging, hammock-like,
drawing deeply on his pipe
and watching his smoke drift about lightly rocking spars,

and he almost expects Jack Chase will be there
waiting for him in the maintop with an easy smile
as in the old days.

But he knows that his tired limbs could not make the climb,
that Jack waits no more in this world,
and that the view would go no farther than Staten Island,
where his brother sits and broods
and stares from the windows of the Sailors' Snug Harbor.

His own journeys now are solely on ferry and cobblestone,
and his only harbor his small hearth,
where each night he gazes into the dwindling flames
and in truth sails far as ever he did,
pushing steadily toward a distant page
on which a handsome sailor, wide-eyed,
hangs by the neck.

WHEN I HEARD THE LEARN'D PROFESSOR
(Walt Visits the English Dept.)

Time avails not and distance avails not, I am with them, the students in English
      365, Section 002, Room 714, Kleingeist Humanities Building,
      MWF 9:10-10:00.

Sitting with the rest, partially stifling yawns with the rest, I wear my cap
      (backwards) indoors or out as I please, though now and again I loose
      my gray locks to the soft, tickling breezes of the central air vents.
Peering over hunched shoulders as the professor speaks of "transgressive
      gender displacement in the Whitmanian text," I see multitudes
      tweeting.
Turning to the ever-sealed window, I look skyward and watch two eagles
      locked tumbling turning in rushing amorous contact. They bring
      me truest tokens of myself.
Rising, I glide through the classroom, sitting briefly beside many I love, feeling
      the negligent leaning of their flesh against my own, casually resting my
      pulsing palm on ample, well-shaped thigh, yet I never tell them a word.
Fingering tiny keys, they stare downward at tiny screens.

Gesturing with handy pocket presentation pointer at the bulleted phrases
      blazoned brightly before him, the professor recites, "'The scent
      of these armpits, aroma finer than prayer.'"
Sniggering, he emphasizes "armpits" and slurs over the lovingly placed
      caesura, over the rich sweet sound of "aroma"; the line, he says,
      "indicative of the early Whitman's privileging of the male body,
      especially his own, so notorious, of course, for its overripe
      odoriferousness."
Smiling archly, he adds, "Perhaps instead of his justly forgotten 'Give Me the
      Splendid Silent Sun' he should have penned 'Give Me the Splendid
      Stick of Right Guard.'"
Smirking, he acknowledges the knowing nods and mirthless chuckles of the
      front-row sycophants (pimple-faced, they are positively not worms
      and fleas).
Pointing his wand once more at a targeted phrase, he grimaces and intones with
      a sneer, "'Not till the sun excludes you, do I exclude you.'"
Shaking his head with studied, urbane bemusement, he marvels, "This line, from
      something called 'To a Common Prostitute', actually strikes many as
      exuding compassion." The front row, similarly bemused, nods with him.

But, "teasing out implications," he perceives "a crude objectification of the
    woman through Walt's appraising, ambiguously male gaze as he
    enhances his self-constructed reputation for generosity of spirit by
    exploiting her as shamelessly as if he were her john."

I once heard America singing—or did I merely sing to myself that I did?
Did I indeed hear varied carols rising as one, though each unique, each
    blithe and strong?

The carpenter dressing his plank, his foreplane's wild lisp ascending. Yes,
    I was there to hear it.
The ringing staccato of anvil and hammer, the aria soaring to the topmost
    balcony, the auctioneer's rhythmic chanting to the sharp-eyed crowd.
    I heard them all.
The grammar school chorus, the cathedral choir, the young mother crooning at
    her cradle, the black hod carriers at their lunch, whistling to fiddle and
    mouth organ. I heard them all.
The high twang, lonesome and loving, of Abraham Lincoln. I heard that, too,
    and hear it yet.

I float through the sealed window, over the campus, the crammed highways,
    the shopping malls.
I sought to bring good fortune to these, my comrades, my sisters, my lovers.
    I sought, yet more, to be good fortune to them, each and all.
But with pods wired to their ears, screens glowing ghostly in their hands, can
    they hear the barbaric yawp I sound, can they think to look for me
    under their bootsoles, where I grow from the grass I love, ready to
    filter and fibre their blood?
Can they search for me up ahead, where I'll stop somewhere waiting for them?

I return briefly to the classroom, where the learn'd professor has moved one
    more point down his list.
Both in and out of the class, both watching and wondering at it, I muse silently,
    amid the fidgeting crowd.
I smile sadly (but not so sadly, after all) and remind myself that, in truth, not till
    the sun excludes them do I exclude any of them, not even the most
    learn'd professor.

GEORGE WASHINGTON WHITMAN WITH WALT IN CAMDEN

I saw Walt's book, didn't read it at all,
didn't think it worth reading,
fingered it a little.
Mother thought as I did—
didn't know what to make of it—
we compared Walt's to *Hiawatha*—
the one was much the same muddle as the other,
except that hunks of Walt's reeked of the whorehouse.
That was 1855, back in Brooklyn, before the War.

Walt wrote that he sometimes ran for sport
down a lane or over fields
while a boy's legs bounced and dangled upon his breast.
I was that boy on his broad shoulders,
laughing and clinging to my big brother.
When I took a bullet at Fredericksburg,
he came south and clung to me,
my big brother still, in the field hospital tent,
till I was fit to fight again.
Then in Washington he tended to others,
a wound-dresser and brother to all,
and kept writing
as he saw the severed arms and legs, still warm,
borne off in trash barrows,
heard the cries, the pleas, the prayers,
smelled the slop buckets' stench,
still no less eager to scrawl his stuff on the page
than he was before the Rebs fired on Sumter,
and the writing still a sad and shameful muddle
from my mother's son, the brother I love.

Meanwhile, I fought till Appomattox—
saw them die at Antietam, Second Bull Run,
Ball's Bluff, New Bern, Chancellorsville,
Fredericksburg, Lynchburg, Petersburg—
an inventory of misery
that Walt might make into one of his long lines.

Maybe I just don't know what a poem is or isn't,
and maybe poor Walt doesn't either.

Since his stroke, he's with Louisa and me in Camden,
each day scribbling pages that few will read.
I say to him, "Walt, why do you do such poems?"
And all he tells me is "I just do what I do
because I do it, that's the whole secret."
And I tell him, "You're stubborner, Walt, than a load of bricks."
And he grins and tells me I know pipes, not poems.
I say that's only as it should be,
since laying lines of flowing pipe in place
is a more weighty matter than laying lines of verse.
He just smiles some more.

Louisa, my dear wife, has suffered—
two infants lost, one named for me,
the other for Walt.
She cared tenderly for Mother,
and now for Walt no less tenderly,
but he is careless of her love,
love her though he does.
Called to dinner last night, he stayed in his tub,
splashing, and singing "When Johnny Comes Marching Home."
Three nights ago, it was "We'll rally 'Round the Flag,"
while we sat 'round the table, Louisa's cooking growing cold,
her eyes smarting with her hurt.

Often, without a word to us,
he hobbles off, his pup Tip at his side,
and rides the Delaware River ferry
back and forth through long afternoons,
coming home at last to speak of the "comrades"
he's chatted with, sung to, and leaned against,
his elbows resting on the rail.
While I inspect the piping for the town,
Walt goes a visitor in his own life.

He's been offered pay
to do more like "O Captain, My Captain,"
(his only poem, truth to tell, I could make out the moral of).
When I suggest he write such things to order,
he just chortles, "We won't talk about that."
I'd tell him he ought to write for folks like Louisa and me,
Americans here and now,
write about our lives and talk and dreams,
so we could understand him
and maybe even enjoy it some,
but I guess he'd just grin again,
and it would be one more thing not to talk about.

I'll never figure him or what he's up to,
but he's my blood and always will be.
I suppose I'll have to read his book through,
one of these days.

Emily's Eyes

Look closely at the picture,
the only one authenticated
as the genuine Emily.
See how the eyes don't align
conventionally, properly.
Each turns from the other,
avoiding binocular resolution.

The name assigned for this
is Exotropic Strabismus,
commonly called Wall Eye.
Each eye is on its own
as it looks sidewise,
away from what is directly before it.

The medical texts tell us
misaligned eyes send separate images.
A child's brain ignores these mixed messages,
resolves them readily into one,
but the adult's may develop Diplopia,
or double vision.
In Emily's case this is extreme.
She may have wished it so—
recall that she told an uncomprehending friend
that she loved to "buffet the sea,"
loved the danger—
this from a woman who'd never boarded ship,
never felt heavy wave
smack against straining planks.
But no danger could have been dearer to her
than that of sailing a true course
in diverging directions
toward a single destination
never to be reached.

Thus, Emily's left eye,
which peers far over your right shoulder,

even as her slightly broad nose
points straight at you,
may be spying that certain slant of light,
the one that weighs so heavy, winter afternoons
(note the downward turn of the lip on that side),
while the right may see,
well past your left shoulder,
a bobolink chirping praise on high
under an orchard's leafy dome
(hence the upward tilt of the lip's right corner?).
The possibilities are many—
the housefly and the hummingbird,
the frost and the flower,
a smile easy as a star and death's stiff stare,
the choiring meeting house,
the silent alabaster chamber.

She wrote that the brain is wider than the sky.
Hers, at any rate, was capacious enough
to hold till the end
a bifurcated vision.
She gave no poem a title,
for she knew no true journey was ever finished,
knew all was ever in tenuous balance,
endless tension.

"Strabismus" is from the Greek for "squinting,"
and though Emily in the photo is wide-eyed,
she peered hard always,
toward something impinging and inevitable
on the very periphery of sight,
far beyond whatever tokens, sinister or sublime,
might be visible at any given moment
to either searching eye.

She knew it was, at last, a wall
that she eyed, and had from the first,
and that, unreachable,
it circumscribed all, enclosed all.
Beyond it, perhaps,
resided an encompassing resolution,
then again, perhaps not.
But still she sailed her double course toward it.

Look more closely now at Emily.
Draw your face, your eyes, close to her own.
Notice, when you're close enough,
that she becomes twin Emilys,
but not quite identical,
one certain that faith is indeed a fine brave thing,
the other no less certain it's an invention,
timid and expedient.
Both Emilys hint at a crooked smile,
as if neither is ever unaware
that the other might be right, after all,
—but only might be.

Pull back a bit now.
Watch the two resolve into Emily,
buffeting the waves,
toward the unattainable wall
that is never beyond her vision.

James Watson, Former Slave

I heard that old Huck Finn had come back
from wherever out West,
worn out and sick,
to be buried in St. Pete.
Maybe knowing at the last
it was Missouri dirt would cover his coffin
satisfied him some.
I don't figure much else ever did,
'cause if all you want is to be let alone,
this world don't offer much in the way of satisfactions.
Tom Sawyer, who wanted 'most everything,
except to leave anyone be,
could've told him that years ago,
if he'd thought to take the time,
but Tom never had much thought nor time
for no one but Tom.
And, truth is, it wouldn't have changed Huck a whit.
That was a haunted boy, eager to be on the move,
like if he stayed in one place too long,
what-all hounded after him would catch hold—
it might have been the wind whisperings,
telling him that wherever he stopped
was the lonesomest place in the world,
or would be if he lingered awhile;
might have been his Pap,
lowest man ever to live on fatback and rotgut;
or it might have been some weepy-heart widow
just aching to make him fit
for what passed for civilization back there and then;
but most of all, clear as I could make it out,
it was the fear he carried close as his shadow
that he was no good and never would be.

I played the darky for him—
didn't have much choice, did I?
I knew what I wanted
(had that much in common with Tom),

and I needed Huck to get it.
Couldn't get nowheres being another Nat Turner,
whatever the gratifications,
so I widened my eyes,
trotted out the hairball and the horse-ass hocus pocus,
all that superstitious crap,
just to keep Huck running with me—
didn't even tell him his Pap was dead
as any doorknob in the house he lay in
floating downriver.
I'm not proud of one bit of that,
But I did try to help him understand some things.
Even if I could have, I wouldn't have cut his throat.

Tom was another story.
At Phelps Farm, I wanted that boy dead,
and I still do.
I was nothing but a dumb black toy to him,
same as my wife and child would have been.
Sure, he was just a kid,
but also the man he'd always be.

I got there just as they were putting Huck in the ground.
Stood off by myself in a stretch of shade,
no one looking my way.
There was just a few folks at the grave,
old-timers not saying much,
except for Tom, that is.
Looking down at the coffin in the hole,
he told them "Years back, Huck was always cheery,
dead eager for a harmless lark and a hearty laugh"
and that "nobody should be too hard on him
for ending up a worthless hobo,
because not everyone has the stuff
to make something of himself."
Someone said Tom was big in the railroad,
had come up from St. Louis in his private Pullman.

His coat was open, and I could see the watch chain
stretched across the tight vest at his swole belly.
The bullet they'd dug out of his leg at Phelps Farm
was hanging from it, just like he'd hung it back then—
the hero and his trophy.
I didn't go near him,
'cause I'd have split him with my blade
and stuck that slug into his open belly,
deep as a seed in a melon.

I knew I owed Huck some honesty.
So, after everybody was gone
and the diggers had done their work,
I went over to the small stone
and told Huck I was sorry
for pretending to be less than I was
and playing him like I did,
said I'd come a long way to tell him that,
all the way from Chicago.
Told him too that me and the wife
sell clothes in our little shop
down on the South Side,
doing all right using everything I learned
as a supply sergeant in Abe Lincoln's army.

I knew he'd be pleased for me
and take my apology right off.
(Maybe he was too soft for this country
and sensed it from the first.)
Then I said, all choked, with tears in my eyes,
that I'm still so mad about so much,
and always will be,
but that the best moments of a bad time
were those I shared with him on the raft,
when, both of us on the run,
we watched the sun ease its way
soft through the mists over the river.

SAM CLEMENS SEES HIS FATHER LAID OPEN

(According to his own account, Clemens secretly watched his
father's autopsy)

The blade slid smoothly, gray throat to gray groin,
the first slice.
Behind the bedroom curtain,
I saw it all, secret, silent, wide-eyed and eleven,
my father's autopsy.
He'd caught a killing cold, out in the sleet,
cadging votes for Clerk of Court,
so desperate to be a somebody,
even in Hannibal,
that here he lay now, nobody.
His last words were of our title
to rocky acres in Tennessee.
"Cling to the land," he said,
"let nothing beguile it away from you."
(Cling to it we did, and it too amounted to nothing.)
But he'd let ambition beguile him from us,
and now a gash, straight as a plough's furrow,
showed the unprofitable soil under the skin.
I peered, glad of my private place,
at this man suddenly so open to view,
yet seeming only barely less sullen
than when he sat among us, muttering his dissatisfactions.
I almost expected to spy worms
crawling through the smeared, clotted lumps
that were his stuffing,
worms thick, white, sluggish and sickly,
nothing like what the dirt of Missouri offered my fish hook.
Had they been there, twisting and toxic,
gnawing in him for years,
diminishing him,
then I could pity him for what ate at me:
his dark glances and darker silences,
his whipping poor, scared little black Jennie,
or selling the weeping Junius and Brutus downriver
for ten barrels of tar.

I wanted to blame worms—
I didn't want to hate him always.
But I didn't see any in my old man
(and no Syph, for that matter,
that Mother had told them to look for,
or so my older brother Orion said later)
and no soul nor spirit either.

All I saw was the stuffing
and the doctor's prying bloody hands
schooling me in the naked truth—
the stuffing itself was all my father was,
all any of us are
right from the start, no more no less,
and men and worms no more pilot their lives
than a log chooses the current that carries it
or than I could choose or not to hate my own father
or to be chilled or not by what I now knew.

And then they sewed it all up
so they could put a suit on him
and show him to the town
for its approval one last time,
the man who might have been
Clerk of Court,
if only he'd been riding a different current.

That was long ago,
but it all stands out clear and sharp
as lightning over the river.

As I lay in bed that night, squinting into the sky,
looking for the vagrant current
that carried in the comet the year I was born
and would carry it back when I'd be old,
I felt as split apart as my father's body.
Glad that I'd bested him,

seen him laid open in his impotence,
and guilty at my gladness.
Certain that Clerk of Court was a paltry thing indeed
beside such titles as I would be borne to,
and no less certain that I was my father's son,
and that rotten stuffing begets rotten stuffing
with all the inevitability of a comet's return.

In my will I'll order that no one cuts me open
on pain of prosecution for trespass.
Besides, I've already done it myself,
each day of my life
since I peered through the curtain.

A GOVERNESS REMEMBERS
(the final turn of the screw)

We were alone with the quiet day,
and Miles' little heart, dispossessed,
had stopped.
Quint had made the child's life a see-saw
of the right throbs and the wrong,
but now all that was over.
I had rescued the boy, bested them both,
the accomplished villain and the half-willing novice.
Still warm, lips parted, showing his small teeth,
Miles hung there, dear troubled thing,
past all troubles now,
clutched in my embrace, a boy finally ever so right,
his feet but inches from the floor.
Careful not to let him fall,
I bent slightly at the knees,
breathing hard,
and brought him up
to lie across my outstretched arms,
then strode down the dark corridors,
my head erect, my eyes bright, my duty done—
the child's soul saved as assuredly
as Quint's was lost, along with the fallen Jessel's.
With what ardent satisfaction
might the devoted uncle on Harley Street
look upon my work!
Rochester, restored at last to sight,
could not have turned upon faithful Jane
an eye more fervent
than my noble employer would turn upon me,
if he could but know.
Poor, dim Mrs. Grose,
seeing me approach bearing my burden and my triumph,
moaned a bovine moan
and fell in a faint, her drool dribbling
on the time-smoothed oaken floor.

I was not much more than a child myself in those days,
yet one far from surprised at my own achievement.
From my earliest years, I'd known
that I'd been shaped (or had shaped myself)
for just such scenes of valor.
Yes, the fluttered, anxious, bookish girl,
fresh from her father's Hampshire vicarage,
who'd presented herself for judgement
at the vast house on Harley Street,
meeching and abject as she might appear
even to her own appraising glance
in the foyer's gilt-framed glass,
knew herself to be equal to any possibility.
And she knew, with no less certainty,
that her prospective employer,
her hoped-for prodigious patron,
handsome and bold and pleasant,
gallant and splendid and kind,
such a figure as had never risen before her,
save in a dream or an old novel,
took her just as she wished to be taken,
knew her just as she wished to be known.
Hence, he proffered her the sacred care of his cherished charges.

And I proved myself indeed equal to it all,
equal to confronting any mystery of Udolpho,
to facing down fifty Quints,
as the great figure on Harley Street
would assuredly have told me
had I ever heard from him again.

But the years since have been little
but chalkboards and tea trays,
lonely chilled walks at dusk,
and silent staring from attic windows,
the wan duration of any mere governess.

I'm mortally certain that each hour
is longer than the one before.
And I fear I'm at last unequal to any of it.
Memory of my triumph at Bly
served for a time, talisman-like,
to fend off the tedious tyranny of the daily,
but now the pendulum's pulse
is fatally ever-slower than my own.

Oh, how I long to see Peter Quint's fierce eyes
gazing ravenously once more into mine
through a mullioned window's warped panes!

Isabel and Lambert at Sea

> "There were some things that had to come in time if they
> were to come at all." *The Ambassadors*

I

By the third day out, they'd noticed each other,
and noticed each other noticing.
Each knew the other was at last, after the long years,
one on whom nothing was lost,
She saw the deep pinch-marks at the bridge of his fine thin nose,
saw the eyes straining to be wry
in the face of privation,
heard him at next table warn a young stranger
of the folly of failing to live all one can,
and watched with him
while the young man stared back stupidly
with all the blankness of youth.
Two ravaged pairs of eyes had met at that moment,
then turned quickly away.

II

Out on deck, in a suit of deep brown,
he stood at the rail and stared eastward,
back toward all he had left,
back toward moments:
eating an *omelette aux tomates* with straw-colored Chablis
in sunshine across the Seine from Notre Dame,
no tomato ever as red, no sun ever as gold,
no flowing river ever as poignant;
scenting in fragrant evening the blooms
and the faint tigerish waft, so perilous, so alluring,
there in the mingled lamplight and shadow,
there in the garden of the formidable Gloriani;
gazing in the dim luster of Marie de Vionnet's drawing-room
at fine *boiseries*, medallions, mouldings, mirrors,
small treasures not numerous but hereditary, cherished, charming,
and at Marie in the midst of them;

touching her shoulder so tentatively, weeks later,
in the same room, dimmer now, less lustrous,
listening to her weep
for Chad, who had told him in listless irritation
that he wasn't tired of her, not a bit, really.
His rarest moments these—never before such glistening promise,
never such defeats,
never such life.
To turn and face west and Woollett just yet
was a bit more than poor Strether could manage,
far harder to face, in fact, than even the memory
of that moment at the country inn,
when the shifting of a parasol in a rowboat
had told all that he had needed and feared to know
of the pair who had made him think himself
so belatedly and blessedly young.

III

From her deck chair, she would look up from her book
and watch him stare fixedly astern.
Now and again she would turn to the west,
toward the land she had left
more than twenty years before,
a place that knew neither Gardencourt nor Roccanera,
that knew neither the grace of sad half-humorous acceptance
nor the vacuity of dreams.
Widowed in essence from the earliest days of her marriage,
she was now, finally, widowed in fact,
the pallor in her thin face, the streaks of gray in her dark hair,
heightened by the deep black of her dress.
She had reached, so hesitantly, for Gilbert's hand
as in his last moments he had looked fixedly
toward his bedroom's frescoed ceiling,
done two centuries before, as he had once told her,
"by some palely-talented dolt with pretensions,

but not done quite so dreadfully as to keep me awake of a night."
The slight twist of his dry lips and merest flinch at his wrist
as her hand drew near,
had told her that even now what he preferred still to grip
was his eternal sense of grievance.
America, he knew, had no patience for what ailed him.
In Rome, remnants of grandeur, lovely accretions of ancient loss
made failure itself a thing of unassailable grace.
Why, then, sail west to all the glare and blare of doing
and leave the satisfactions of silence and shadow?
So, over the stale decades, Gilbert had stayed, and she with him.
Oh, yes, she'd often thought of home,
and often thought of it in fear,
dreading to find there, around every corner,
the girl who had read so many books
and had dreamed so many dreams of Europe and glory.
Now she was at last ready to face that girl,
to stare at her as fixedly as one might stare at the embers
of a failing fire in a large chilled house,
and muse on the general sadness of things.

IV

It rained all their last day at sea,
but shortly before dark, it eased to drizzle.
and each came out alone and stood at the rail,
staring into the shifting mist and the slow churning below.
Not ten feet separated them, that and the silence.
They stood there in the chill and in their thoughts,
all the rest inside in the warm clatter of table chat.
After a time, the two turned to each other,
as if by common need.
Some words of the weather, the pleasantness of the voyage,
the likely hour of arrival,
while their eyes met and held.
Their smiles, at first hesitant, grew warmer

in mutual understanding.
They knew and knew.
They might have walked the deck together
through the long evening, exchanged addresses
and sincere promises to meet in their homeland
and see what they could make of it together.
After all, he was but fifty-seven, and she just in her forties,
and both knowledgeable of possibilities.
But they didn't—for, after all,
each had seen too much of what comes of possibilities,
and there they were.
So, after they watched the sun sink wanly
through drizzle and mist, they merely smiled once more,
wished each other a not uncomfortable night
and a not unhappy return.

Henry James Strolls the Lower East Side

(suggested by James's account in *The American Scene* of New
York's recent Jewish immigrants)

The street seemed some vast, sallow aquarium,
innumerable fish of over-developed proboscis,
a great swarming, thickening infinitely,
bumping together, forever,
amid heaped spoils of the sea—
and there is no swarming like that of Israel
when once Israel has got a start.

But, of course, no thick glass shielded him,
nor did his capacity for metaphor.
Resolutely, our troubled observer
moved among them in their element,
the solidity of the sidewalk beneath him
reminding him this was in fact the city
he had once known so well.

This place was for them, at last,
the New Jerusalem:
the promised pavements
where they might mill and push
among the over-piled carts
the spilling garbage cans,
the dribbling hydrants and greasy gutters.
Visages, each with the whole hard glitter of their tribe,
peered from narrow tenement windows,
from mattresses spread on fire escapes
and through storefront glass smeared
with the painted cost of things.

He thought of John Winthrop staring westward
from the bow of the *Arbella*,
dreaming of a city on a hill;
This, though, was both present and future,
unmistakable and immitigable,

the legacy of Concord and Lexington
descending to the scourings of the east.

Isabel Archer, Milly Theale,
poor perplexed Strether,
landing here again,
would sail promptly back to Europe,
exiled from all but their memories
of a place once dear to them.

Seated now with a cup of turbid tea
set before him on a sticky oilcloth,
the stale bun beside it oozing strange nastiness
onto a chipped plate,
he watched men with collars frayed and grimy
suck tea through sugar cubes
gripped between yellowed teeth.
In each visage, the gathered Hebraic past
untempered by time or place.

A youngish man, thin, drawn, unshaven,
glanced his way, glanced again,
stared, and approached, holding a book.
He smiled shyly, bobbed his head in an attempt at a bow,
and said, "Are you Mr. Henry James?
I haf seen a picture of you."
James nodded and replied, "I am, sir,"
sensing immediately that the moment bristled
with possibilities for wry anecdote.
"This I cannot believe," the fellow said,
"for only today I finished your *Vings of the Dove*,
vhich I haf here in mine hand.
I read it late into the nights after mine vork
and at lunchtimes beside mine sewing machine.
Vhen that Mr. Densher and Miss Croy,
gave up everything

because they vas ashamed over vhat they had done,
I just shook mine head
at how vell you show vhat it is to be a human being."
And holding out his book hesitantly,
he asked, "Vould you mind to please sign your name?
It vould mean to me more
than vhat I can tell to you."

James signed,
then watched as the fellow,
after bowing once more, walked off,
Seeing how close to himself
the fellow held his book,
James shook his own head,
removed his pince nez
and wiped his eyes.

Edna Pontellier Undrowned

The old dog chained to the sycamore strained at her tether
and barked into the Mississippi spring.
The dignified, sad-eyed cavalry officer strode across the porch,
his spurs clanging echoes of ancient battle
as they struck the warped boards.
The bees hummed amid the musk-scented pinks.
I took the whole delicious Whitmanian inventory
of the dreamy afternoons of my youth,
as I swam far out into the Gulf.

Leonce, Adele, even Robert,
with his puling "Good by—because I love you,"
myopic creatures of *les convenances*—
had any of them seen such afternoons,
dreamed my dreams?

The sea's touch was sensuous,
enfolding my body in its soft embrace,
so I closed my eyes and let myself sink gratefully
into the deep endless meadows of childhood.
Tall leafy grasses swayed gently
in the light breeze of a sonata by Schubert,
each note supple, serene, solacing,
each meant for me alone,
utterly delicious.
Ah, si tu savais!

Then I saw it was Reisz at the keyboard,
watched her turn and sneer through yellowed barracuda teeth,
"And you call yourself an artist, Madame!"
and I awoke with a gasp to my own drowning
and the taste of brine.

I stretched again and again for the shore,
the lilt of the sonata lost in my frantic panting
and the steady din of the surf.

That din echoes only faintly now.
More vibrant is the el train's chugging overhead
while daily I walk the city,
my camera, ever at hand, my only companion.
I give myself to New York fully,
and in return it offers itself to my lens.
Some indeed call me artist now,
and I assure them that their praise is, of course, delicious;
but what matters are my pictures,
more my children, truly, than Etienne and Raoul,
and I dote on them no less than Adele on her brood.
The men with whom I choose to sleep
please me well enough,
but never so much as my camera.

Sometimes I see Reisz's wizened visage in a dream.
I smile upon it fondly, and she seems to smile back,
a look worthy of a picture.

Louisiana thinks me lost in the Gulf.
Let it think so. We're both the better for it.
Last week I glimpsed Leonce walking near Wall Street,
peering in a journal as he went,
and no doubt eager to get home to those he knows.

As for me, last Sunday, I sat in Central Park,
recalled the cavalry officer's spurs, the dog under the sycamore,
the bees' hum, the smell of the pinks,
and knew that the girl in their midst
saw her way through to the stuff of her dreams.

LEONCE PONTELLIER, WIDOWER

When they told me of her last swim, I was sad, of course.
The carton with her clothes, grains of sand still clinging—
how often I'd seen her garments spread across a bedroom chair!
No doubt, though, she gave herself naked to the sea
more willingly than she'd given herself to me that summer.
The water her final day was choppy and chill,
the undercurrents treacherous,
her swim ill-advised from the start, the coroner said.
An accident, he judged, and so the papers duly noted,
one acquaintance (unnamed) lamenting her "impulsiveness,"
which "some said had been increasing of late."
"Suicide" went unspoken in my presence,
though not in my speculations.
But even suicide takes forethought,
so an accident it must have been,
as her notions rarely took definite shapes—
it must have been a heedless moment's hectic fancy
that in the depths of the Gulf
she would find all that had eluded her
as Mrs. Edna Pontellier.
Such impetuousness run amuck
is not infrequent among females of a certain sort.

And Edna was of that certain sort,
more eager to yearn than to have,
never satisfied to be in place,
ever gazing intently into the distance,
while I squinted through my thick lenses
at the cotton quotes in agate type.

She married me in defiance of Mississippi.
Catholic New Orleans Creole,
I was for her at first an intoxicating exotic,
a (bespectacled) Lochinvar
carrying her off far from her family's displeasure

(so essential to her vision)
to the unbounded realms of indefinite grandeur
her girlish dreams had conjured.

But soon she saw I was but Leonce Pontellier,
commodities broker,
and New Orleans, for all its allurements,
was but an address in this world.
Thus her visions went a-glimmering,
like the faint glow of fireflies at first gray of dawn.
And she slipped into a dreamless somnolence.
To say she seemed more sleepwalker than spouse
is unkind to her memory, yet not far wide of the mark.

And I was never less than dutiful,
as provider, father, and (often baffled) husband.
Nor did I frequent the barrooms and bordellos
any more often than others of my circle.
My thoughts did occasionally turn,
I must admit, to the blond and buxom Adele,
so warmly content as wife, mother, and neighbor,
unlike my angular and listless Edna,
but I'm not a chap inconsiderate of the proprieties,
and so I brought my thoughts to heel.

Raoul once asked if Edna were really his mother.
I told him not to be foolish.
But how indeed could he and poor little Etienne
not wonder about a woman so distant and distracted,
and when her swimming that summer stirred her dormant dreams
to a troubling wakefulness,
what indeed could any of us make of her?
Now their memories of her grow hazy,
dwindling fragments of a troubled night
from which they have gratefully wakened.

I missed her for a time.
There was something a bit piquant, of course,
in those far-gazing eyes and that yearning look,
but, frankly, how long can a man miss a woman
who viewed him as a bit of a bore?

I'm seeing someone lately.
The boys like her, and she dotes on them already.
A Creole, she gets on well with my circle.
She wears glasses, and, once, for a joke,
we switched spectacles with each other.
Each saw clearly through the other's lenses.

Last week, in New York, near Wall Street, on business,
I saw a woman glancing about, camera in hand,
who seemed a near image of Edna.
I peered into my paper till I'd left her sight,
then looked around with satisfaction,
at the substantial street,
rather than into the unsettled face of dreams.

Henry Fleming's Faded Red Badge

Showing my teeth and snarling curses,
hunched low like a fullback,
I grabbed the flag from a falling lad
and led the smoky way
toward the fire-flashing gray lines.

Later, men patted my soaked back,
and my colonel smiled
and called me wildcat.

That was my first fight,
Chancellorsville,
Fifty years gone yonder now.

The Johnnies whipped us that day,
but for me that mattered little.
As we slogged off through liquid mud,
weary and wet under a wretched sky,
my shoulders were squared,
my jaw set, and my prospects bright,
for I saw this world was a world for me.
My bandaged brow throbbed
a drumbeat pulsing my pride
at what I'd done before others' eyes.

And what none had seen,
that I never told—
I'd skedaddled early on
as Stonewall's Rebs swept toward me,
howling through the morning mists.
Later, seeing a squirrel scamper
from my shied pinecone,
I assured myself
I'd simply followed Nature's law.
It seemed no less natural, I suppose,
when I soon left my tattered comrade

babbling and bleeding
in the tall weeds beside the road.
Of these I never spoke.

After Appomattox,
I marched home a hero
and through a half-century
of days and nights.
Seeing me working my fields,
folks still salute as they ride by.
Sitting at the cracker barrel
and pot belly stove in town,
they hear and nod as I speak,
a local vestige of ancient glory.
My sons' sons ask about the war,
and their eyes go wide
as I tell of Gettysburg, Petersburg,
and that charge at Chancellorsville.
Of what preceded, I never tell
and never will.

The time for telling came and went.
And I hold my head as high
as ever I did that day I marched off
through the mud and the cold,
warmed by memories of those pats on the back
and the echoing voice saying "wildcat."

Too many nights, though, near dawn,
I hear things in the breeze—
bugle calls,
men and horses making ready,
far off across my meadow
in the dark of the tree line.
And I know that the tattered man is there,
and those that stood their ground and died

while I fled
and tossed pine cones at a squirrel.
I stare out my window
till they leave with the sunrise.
They will never charge;
no, they wait for me to bare my breast
and rush wildly to them,
their strayed comrade.
I never will.
Defeated each time, I return to bed,
my eyes smarting in the morning glare,
soon to endure another day in my march,
another day with shoulders squared
and head held high.

What ever made me think
this world was one for me?

YOUNG EDITH NEWBOLD JONES WHARTON TAKES UP HER PEN

One was polite, considerate of others;
such were the principles of the well-bred.
Bad manners were the worst offense—
so Edith Newbold Jones was taught from the first.
But with hands and feet large as a laborer's,
hair red as an Irish servant-girl's,
skin pasty and pimply as any street urchin's,
and lips thin, pinched, and unpromising,
she was inconsiderate enough
to be homely in her handsome family,
not to keep up, as it were,
with her fellow Joneses.
And she was taught thoroughly to know that, too,
most of all by her beautiful well-bred mother.

Caught, as she recalled,
in a "perpetual cross-fire of criticism,"
she told her aunt she dreamed of becoming
the "best-dressed woman in New York."
But, watching her fashionable mother
smile vacuously into the dressmaker's mirror,
she turned quickly to other dreams,
ones of her own devising.

Thus, she took to "making up,"
as she called it—
not with lipstick, rouge, or powder,
but with pencil on paper—
scribbling stories, many of them,
none about unhappy, homely little girls.

Mother, though, refusing to indulge bad habits,
allowed her no stationery,
which, after all, cost money
that might be spent on clothes—

so Edith wrote on large sheets
of used wrapping paper,
spread wide on the floor,
put, she hoped, to better use
than when it held Mother's purchases.

Her parents, she later wrote,
began to regard her with fear,
seeing a pale predestined child,
her unsettled mind,
given to obscure departures
and erratic returns,
over-eager to share
the dubious fruits of her journeys,
the ill-conceived creatures
of her "making-up."
On maternal principle, then,
as much as good taste,
her beautiful mother observed disdainfully
one's drawing room is *always* tidy,
when the bothersome girl
wrote of one whose drawing room *wasn't*.
She showed her mother no more stories.

And, later on, the predestined child
conceived of lives far less tidy
than drawing rooms,
of offences worse than bad manners
or even than homeliness.

Her Lily Bart, lovely as any mother might wish,
dead in an untidy rented room,
a faded flower, tossed aside by fashion;
her Newland Archer, forlorn and loveless,
plodding the daily round of duty,
just as his social station *would* have it;

her Ethan Frome, hag-ridden
by both wife and lover,
by fate itself, it seemed,
caught in a crossfire of criticism,
in the coldest and grayest of wastelands.

Life, thin, pinched, and unpromising,
was lived out in her pages.
No other outcome imaginable
to the child with a laborer's hands
who built a career on "making up."

As her mother might have said,
"breeding tells."

ACKNOWLEDGMENTS

"Virginia Poe Dying" has appeared in *The Roanoke Review*. "Isabel and Lambert at Sea" and "Young Edith Newbold Jones Takes Up Her Pen" have appeared in *Modern Age*. "James Watson, Former Slave" appeared in *The South Carolina Review*. "Bartleby's last Speech" appeared in *Leviathan, the Journal of Melville Studies*. "Edna Pontellier, Undrowned" and "Leonce Pontellier, Widower" appeared in *Juked*. "Ralph Waldo Emerson Meets John Brown" appeared in *Chronicles: A Magazine of American Culture*. "Emily's Eyes" appeared in *Lost Coast*, "Henry Fleming's Faded Red Badge" in *War, Literature & the Arts*, and "Herman Melville, Customs Inspector 188" in *The Delmarva Review*.

About the Author

Allen Stein was born in the Bronx and has taught American Literature at North Carolina State University since 1968. His numerous essays on American writers have appeared in such journals as *American Literature*, *American Literary Realism*, and *Modern Language Quarterly*. He has also published books on the short fiction of Kate Chopin and on the portrayal of marriage in the works of American Literary Realists. His poems and stories have appeared in *The Hudson Review*, *Poet Lore*, *Salmagundi*, and *Willow Springs*, among other literary magazines, and his first poetry collection, *Your Funeral is Very Important to Us*, appeared in 2019.

Book designed by Larry W. Moore
for Broadstone Books,
using Baskerville Old Face,
printed in a limited edition
on permanent paper
by Bookmobile